the BIG Christmas

COLORING BOOK for TODDLERS

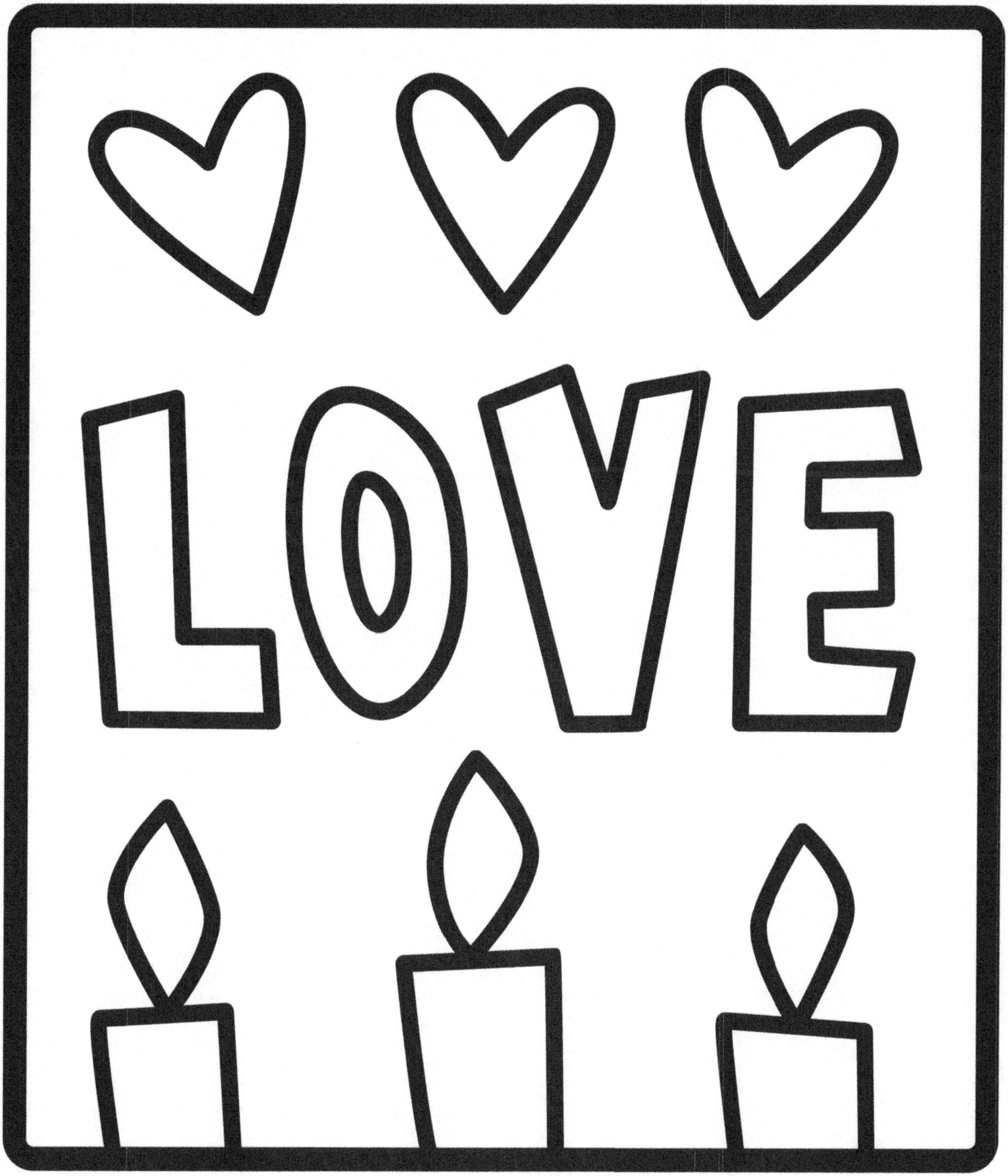
LOVE

DECORATE THE TREE!

Happy Winter!

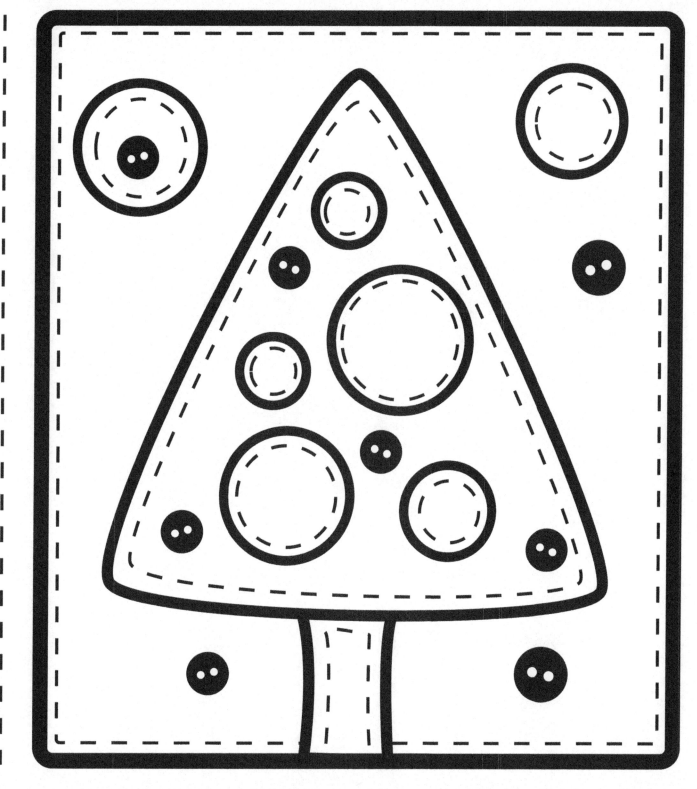

DECORATE THE TREE!

cactus tree

DECORATE THE ORNAMENTS!

SNOWFLAKE

DECORATE THE SNOWMAN!

CANDY CANE

CANDY CANE

CANDY CANE

merry x-mas

palm tree

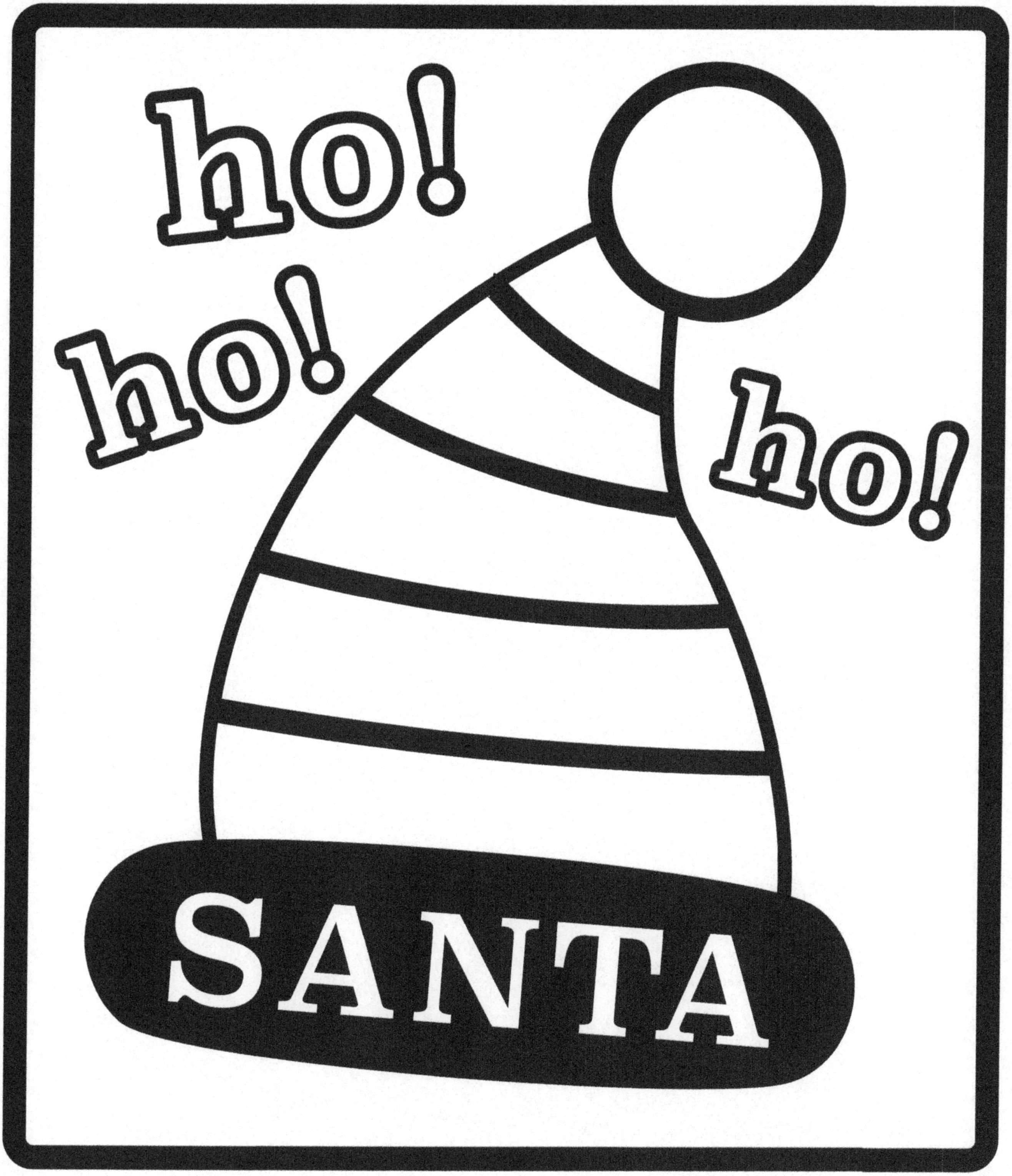
ho!
ho!
ho!
SANTA

DECORATE THE STOCKING!

SNOWFLAKE

DECORATE THE TREE!

UNICORN SNOWMAN!

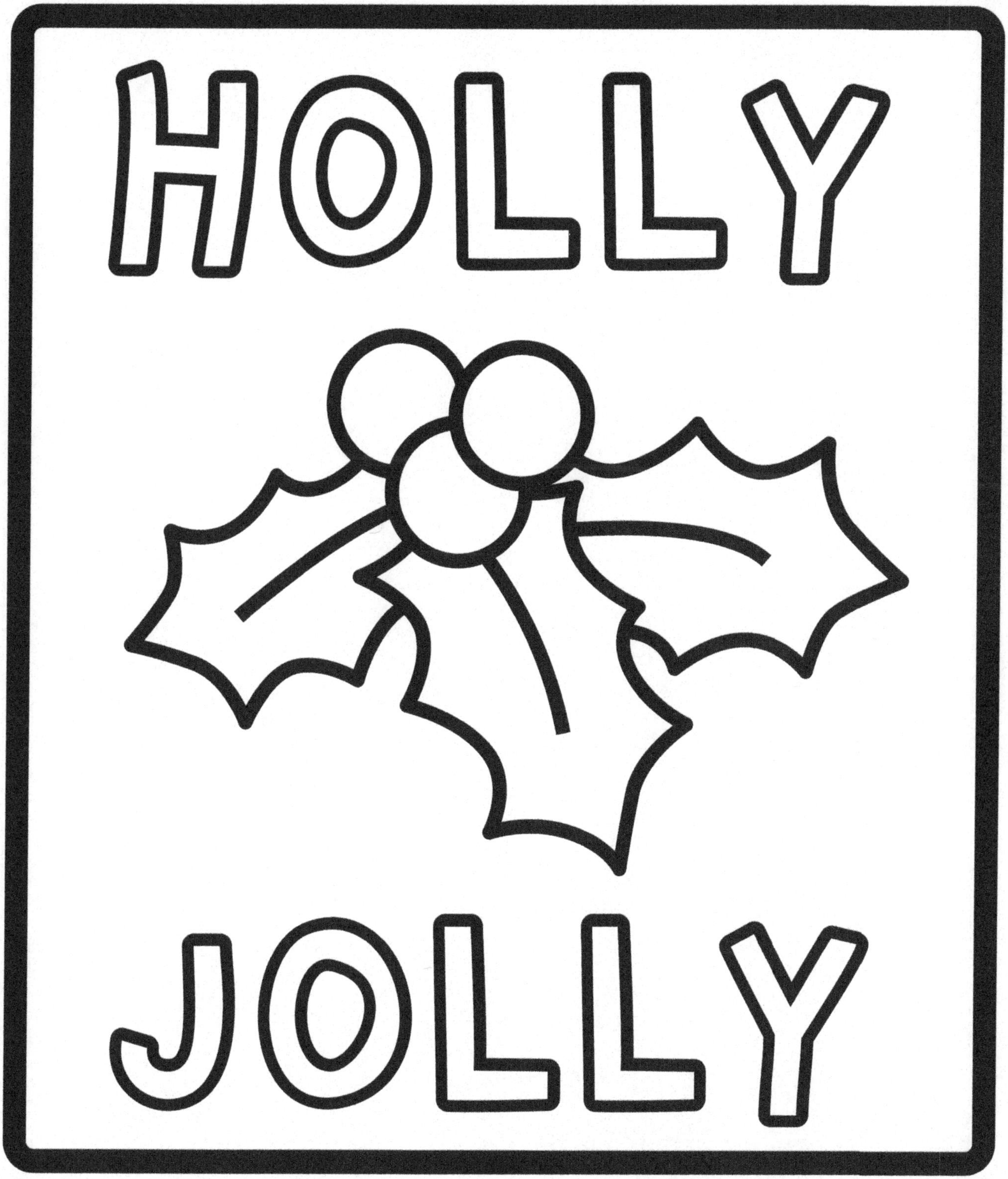
HOLLY
JOLLY

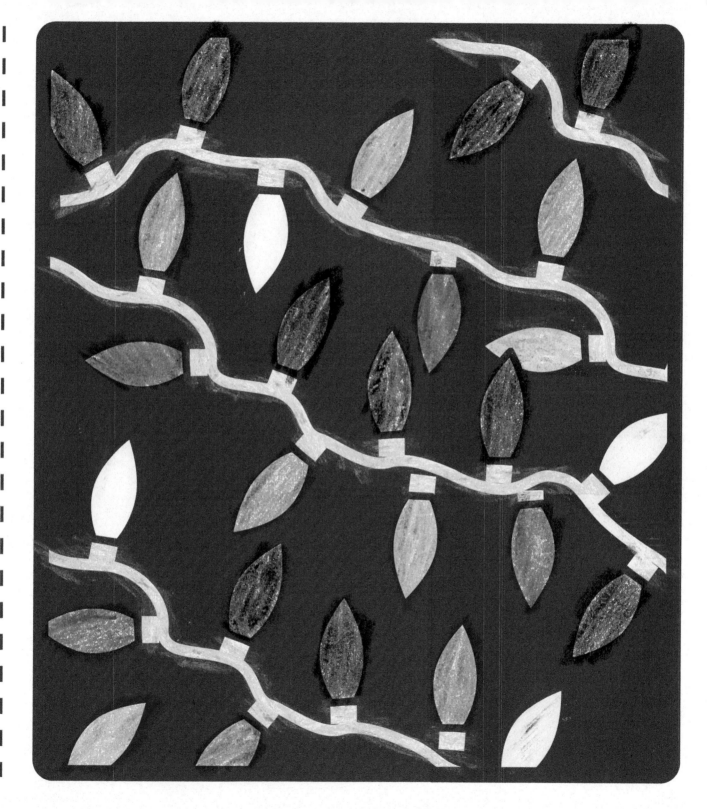

DECORATE THE STOCKING!

SNOWFLAKE

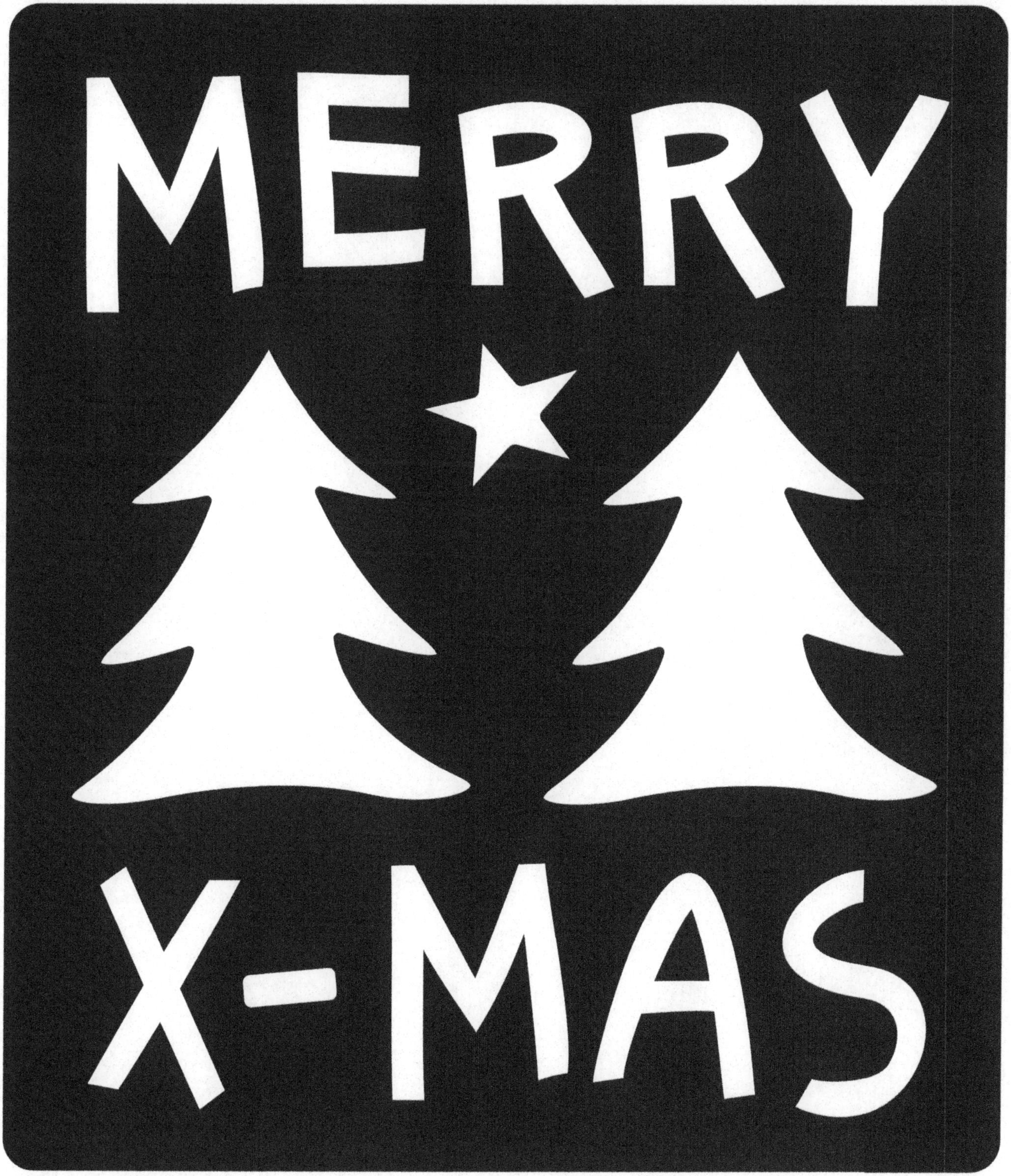
MERRY
X-MAS

DECORATE THE ORNAMENTS!

SNOW MAN!

CANDY CANE

CANDY CANE

CANDY CANE

DECORATE THE TREE!

DECORATE THE ORNAMENTS!

DECORATE THE SNOWMAN!

DECORATE THE TREE!

Made in the USA
Coppell, TX
25 November 2020

42106385R00057